Differentiated Reading
for Comprehension

Grade 3

Credits
Content Editor: Jennifer B. Stith
Copy Editor: Karen Seberg
Illustrations: Nick Greenwood, Donald O'Connor

Visit *carsondellosa.com* for correlations to Common Core, state, national, and Canadian provincial standards.

Carson-Dellosa Publishing, LLC
PO Box 35665
Greensboro, NC 27425 USA
carsondellosa.com

Table of Contents

Introduction

Providing all students access to high quality, nonfiction text is essential to Common Core State Standards mastery. This book contains exactly what teachers are looking for: high-interest nonfiction passages, each written at three different reading levels, followed by a shared set of text-dependent comprehension questions and a writing prompt to build content knowledge. Both general academic and domain-specific vocabulary words are reinforced at the end of each passage for further comprehension support. The standards listed on each page provide an easy reference tool for lesson planning, and the Common Core Alignment Chart on page 3 allows you to target or remediate specific skills.

The book is comprised of 15 stories that are written at three levels:
- Below level (one dot beside the page number): 1 to 1.5 levels below grade level
- On level (two dots beside the page number): 0 to .5 levels below grade level
- Advanced (three dots beside the page number): 1 to 2 levels above grade level

Which students will not enjoy reading about an egg-laying mammal or a man who cooked eggs on a tightrope over Niagara Falls or a place where a person's breath freezes into ice crystals? This book will quickly become the go-to resource for differentiated nonfiction reading practice in your classroom!

Common Core Alignment Chart

Common Core State Standards*		Practice Pages
Reading Standards for Informational Text		
Key Ideas and Details	3.RI.1–3.RI.3	7, 11, 15, 19, 23, 27, 31, 35, 39, 43, 47, 51, 55, 59, 63
Craft and Structure	3.RI.4–3.RI.6	4–6, 8–10, 12–14, 16–18, 20–22, 24–26, 27, 28–30, 31, 32–34, 35, 36–38, 40–42, 44–46, 48–50, 52–54, 55, 56–58, 59, 60–62, 63
Integration of Knowledge and Ideas	3.RI.7–3.RI.9	15, 27, 31, 35, 55, 59, 63
Range of Reading and Level of Text Complexity	3.RI.10	4–6, 8–10, 12–14, 16–18, 20–22, 24–26, 28–30, 32–34, 36–38, 40–42, 44–46, 48–50, 52–54, 56–58, 60–62
Reading Standards: Foundational Skills		
Phonics and Word Recognition	3.RF.3	19, 23, 43, 47, 59
Fluency	3.RF.4	4–6, 8–10, 12–14, 16–18, 20–22, 24–26, 28–30, 32–34, 36–38, 40–42, 44–46, 48–50, 52–54, 56–58, 60–62
Writing Standards		
Text Types and Purposes	3.W.1–3.W.3	7, 11, 15, 19, 23, 27, 31, 39, 43, 47, 51, 59, 63
Production and Distribution of Writing	3.W.4–3.W.6	47, 51
Language Standards		
Conventions of Standard English	3.L.1–3.L.2	7, 19, 23, 35, 39, 43, 47, 51, 55, 63
Knowledge of Language	3.L.3	7
Vocabulary Acquisition and Use	3.L.4–3.L.6	4–6, 7, 8–10, 11, 12–14, 16–18, 20–22, 24–26, 27, 28–30, 32–34, 36–38, 39, 40–42, 43, 44–46, 48–50, 51, 52–54, 56–58, 60–62

How to Use This Alignment Chart

The Common Core State Standards for English Language Arts are a shared set of expectations for each grade level in the areas of reading, writing, speaking, listening, and language. They define what students should understand and be able to do. This chart presents the standards that are covered in this book.

Use this chart to plan your instruction, practice, or remediation of a specific standard. To do this, first choose your targeted standard; then, find the pages listed on the chart that correlate to the standard you are teaching. Finally, assign the reading pages and follow-up questions to practice the skill.

The Egg-Laying Mammal

People first thought the platypus was a joke. They thought someone had put a duck's bill on a beaver's body! They saw other odd things. The animal had webbed feet. It had short legs like a lizard's. It had two layers of fur. It had a **spur** on each of its back leg. What kind of animal was this?

The platypus lives in Australia. It is a **mammal** that lays eggs. It lives under the ground. It spends a lot of time in water. A platypus goes in the water many times in an hour to get food. Its webbed feet and flat tail help it swim. It catches worms, snails, and shrimp. It carries food in its cheeks. The platypus does not have teeth. It has little pads inside its bill that grind its food.

This animal is furry and brown. It is about the size of a house cat. It lives about as long as a cat too. Its babies are called puggles. The puggles hatch out of eggs. The mother platypus feeds them milk. The babies live in a **burrow**. Platypuses make burrows on the banks of rivers or streams.

Only the male platypus has spurs. It uses its spurs like stingers. It can sting other animals in a fight. An animal can die from the sting. Humans do not die from the sting. They can get very sick. People learned to leave this odd animal alone!

spur: a sharp spine
mammal: an animal that feeds milk to its young
burrow: a nest in the ground

The Egg-Laying Mammal

When people in England first saw a stuffed platypus, they thought it was a joke. They thought someone had put a duck's bill on a beaver's body! Then, they saw other strange things. The platypus had webbed feet. It had short legs like a lizard's. It had two layers of fur. And, it had a **spur** on each of its back leg. What kind of animal was this?

The platypus lives in Australia. It is one of the strangest animals in the world. For one thing, it lays eggs, even though it is a **mammal**. It lives underground, but it spends a lot of time in the water. A platypus dives in the water up to 80 times an hour to get food. Its webbed feet and flat tail help it swim. It catches worms, snails, and shrimp. It carries food in its cheeks until it is ready to eat. The platypus does not have teeth. It has little pads inside its bill that grind its food.

This furry brown animal is about the size of a house cat. It lives about as long as a cat too—10 to 17 years. Its babies are called puggles. They hatch out of their eggs. The mother platypus feeds them milk. The babies live in a **burrow** that is built with long tunnels for doorways. Platypuses make burrows on the banks of rivers or streams. This lets them hunt for food easily.

Only the male platypus has spurs that it uses like stingers. It uses its spurs in fighting. When another animal is stung, it can die. Humans do not die from the sting of a platypus. But, they do get very sick. The poison in a spur causes great pain. People in Australia learned to leave this odd animal alone!

spur: a sharp spine
mammal: an animal that feeds milk to its young
burrow: a nest in the ground

The Egg-Laying Mammal

When people in England first saw a stuffed platypus, they thought it was a joke. They thought someone had glued a duck's bill on a beaver's body! Then, they noticed other strange features. The platypus had webbed feet and short legs like a lizard's. It had two layers of fur. It had **spurs** on each of its back leg. What kind of animal was this?

The platypus lives in Australia. It is one of the strangest animals in the world. For one thing, it lays eggs, even though it is a **mammal**. It lives underground, but it spends a lot of time in the water. A platypus dives in the water up to 80 times an hour to get food. Its webbed feet and flat tail help it swim. It catches worms, snails, and shrimp. It carries food in pouches in its cheeks until it is ready to eat. The platypus does not have teeth. It has little pads inside its bill that grind its food.

This furry brown animal is about the size of a house cat. It lives about as long as a cat too—10 to 17 years. Its babies, called puggles, hatch from eggs and then the mother platypus feeds them milk. The babies live in a **burrow** that is built with long tunnels for doorways. Platypuses make burrows on the banks of rivers or streams. This lets them hunt for food easily.

Only the male platypus has spurs that it uses like stingers. It uses the spur in fighting or in defense. When another animal is stung, it can die. Humans do not die from the sting of a platypus. But, they do get very sick. The poison in a spur causes great pain that no medicine can make better. Settlers in Australia quickly learned to leave this funny-looking animal alone!

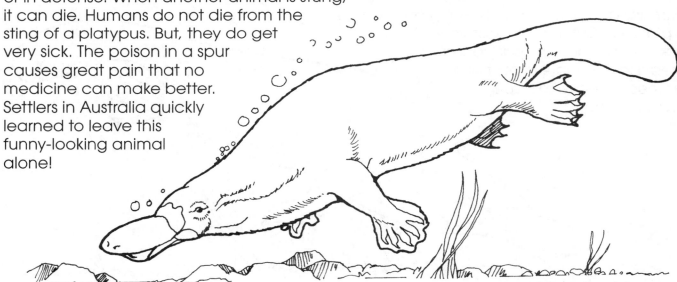

spur: a sharp spine
mammal: an animal that feeds milk to its young
burrow: a nest in the ground

The Egg-Laying Mammal

Answer the questions.

1. Read the following sentence from the story and answer the question.

   Platypuses make burrows on the banks of rivers or streams.

   Which definition of the word *banks* matches the way it is used in the story?

   A. places to keep money

   B. sets of cards used in games

   C. groups of clouds

   D. sloped grounds on the edge of a body of water

2. What is a *puggle*? Write your answer in a complete sentence.

   _____

   _____

3. Which of the following is not a feature of the platypus?

   A. a bill like a duck's

   B. a body like a beaver's

   C. paws like a dog's

   D. short legs like a lizard's

4. Which of the following behaviors is not typical of a mammal?

   A. swimming in water

   B. laying eggs

   C. fighting other animals

   D. digging holes

5. Complete the sentence.

   It has _____ _____ inside its _____ that grind its _____.

6. Which sentence shows commas used correctly?

   A. It catches, worms snails and shrimp.

   B. It catches worms, snails and, shrimp.

   C. It catches worms snails, and shrimp.

   D. It catches worms, snails, and shrimp.

7. Read this sentence.

   I saw a platypus at the zoo.

   Rewrite the sentence to make it more exciting. Add details and adjectives.

   _____

8. When people first saw the platypus, they thought it was a joke. On another sheet of paper, write about a time you saw something that you thought was a joke. Choose words carefully to make the story interesting and even funny.

The King of the Frogs

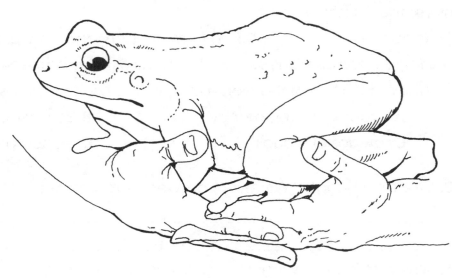

Frogs come in many sizes. The smallest frog in the world is less than one-half inch (7.7 mm) long. That is the size of a housefly. This frog has a very big cousin. It is the goliath frog. It is the biggest frog in the world.

The goliath frog only lives in one place. This place is on the western **coast** of Africa. The goliath frog's body is almost one foot (30.48 cm) long. When its legs are stretched, they are about two feet (60.96 cm) long! The goliath frog can weigh up to seven pounds (3.18 kg). That is about as big as a house cat.

People from Europe did not even know about this frog until 1906. It must have been a big surprise to see a frog that size! People who live in the **rain forest** of West Africa have known about the goliath frog. They use the frog for both meat and medicine.

The goliath frog is brown and green. It lives in rivers and streams. It likes water that moves fast. It catches fish to eat. The frog can jump 10 feet (3.05 m) at a time.

Some people trap the goliath frog. In the United States, people used to have frog-jumping **contests**. Goliath frogs would be brought to the United States for these contests. Some people want to keep goliath frogs as pets. These big frogs can die when they are taken away from the rain forest.

coast: the land near a sea or ocean
rain forest: an area of tall trees that receives a lot of rain
contest: event that ends with a winner

The King of the Frogs

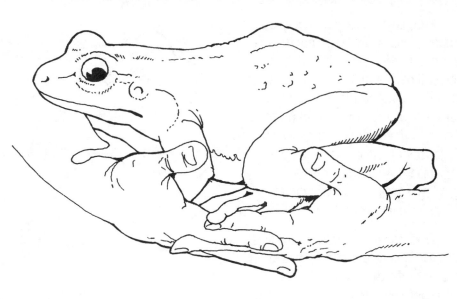

Frogs come in many sizes and colors. Some frogs are so bright in color that they look like toys! The smallest frog in the world is less than one-half inch (7.7 mm) long. That is the size of a housefly. This frog has a very big cousin in Africa. It is the goliath frog, the biggest frog in the world.

The goliath frog only lives in one place on the western coast of Africa. Its body is almost one foot (30.48 cm) long. When its legs are **extended**, they are about two feet (60.96 cm) long! The goliath frog can weigh up to seven pounds (3.18 kg). This frog is about as big as a house cat.

Explorers from Europe did not even know about this frog until 1906. It must have been a big **shock** to see a frog that size! Of course, people who live in the rain forest have known about the goliath frog all along. They use the frog for both meat and medicine.

The brownish-green goliath frog lives in rivers and streams. It likes fast-moving water. It catches fish and shellfish to eat. When it is in danger, the frog can use its long back legs to jump 10 feet (3.05 m) at a time.

Hunters in the area still trap the goliath frog and so do hunters from other parts of the world. In the United States, people once had frog-jumping **contests**. Goliath frogs would be brought across the sea for these contests. Today, some people want goliath frogs as pets. But, these huge frogs often die when they are taken away from their rain forest homes.

extended: stretched to full size or length
shock: a sudden disturbance
contest: event that ends with a winner

The King of the Frogs

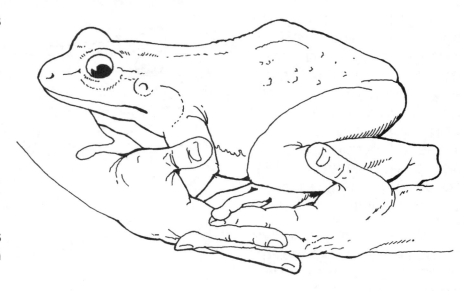

Frogs come in many sizes and colors. Some frogs are so bright in color that they look like toys! The smallest frog in the world is less than one-half inch (7.7 mm) long. That is the size of a housefly. This frog has a very large cousin in Africa. It is the goliath frog, the biggest frog in the world.

The goliath frog only lives in one place on the western coast of Africa. Its body is almost one foot (30.48 cm) long. When its legs are **extended**, they are about two feet (60.96 cm) long! The goliath frog can weigh up to seven pounds (3.18 kg), which is about as big as a house cat.

Explorers from Europe did not even know this frog existed until 1906. It must have been a **shock** to see a frog of that size! Of course, **native** people who live in the rain forests of the western coast of Africa have known about the goliath frog all along. They use the frog for both food and medicine.

The goliath frog is brownish-green in color. It lives in fast-moving rivers and streams. The goliath frog catches fish and shellfish to eat. When it is in danger, the frog can use its long back legs to jump 10 feet (3.05 m) at a time.

Hunters in the area still trap the goliath frog and so do hunters from other parts of the world. In the United States, people once had frog-jumping contests. Goliath frogs would be brought across the ocean for these **contests**. Today, some people want goliath frogs as pets. But, these huge frogs often die when they are taken away from their rain forest homes.

extended: stretched to full size or length
shock: a sudden disturbance
native: local; belonging to a place or region
contest: event that results in a winner; competitions

The King of the Frogs

Answer the questions.

1. Read the following sentence from the story and answer the question.

   The smallest frog in the world is less than one-half inch (7.7 mm) long.

   Why do you think the author included this fact?

   A. so that the reader could learn more about small frogs

   B. so that the reader could learn about every frog in the world

   C. so that the reader can compare the smallest and biggest frogs

   D. so that the reader could learn about goliath frogs

2. Which of the following sentences best sums up the main idea of the story?

   A. Goliath frogs are only one kind of frog in the world.

   B. The largest frog in the world is the goliath frog from Africa.

   C. The goliath frog is the size of a large house cat.

   D. The goliath frog likes to live in fast-moving water.

3. Why is the goliath frog trapped?

   A. for food

   B. to be a pet

   C. for medicine

   D. all of the above

Complete each sentence.

4. When it is in danger, the goliath frog can jump _____ at a time.

5. When you add the length of the goliath frog's body and legs, it is almost
   _____ long.

6. People once brought goliath frogs to enter in _____ contests.

7. Do you think that the goliath frog would make a good pet? Why or why not? Write
   your answer on another sheet of paper.

The Leopard That Went for Help

Billy Arjan Singh lives on a farm in India. He takes care of animals. Billy takes in big cats like leopards and tigers that do not have a mother or father.

One **orphan** cub was a leopard named Harriet. Billy taught Harriet how to go back and live in the wild. He built tree platforms to teach her how to climb. He took her on walks in the forest. He showed her how to hunt.

Finally, Harriet was ready to go live in the forest. Billy rowed her across a river to the trees. She got out of the boat. She went into the forest on her own. Billy kept track of Harriet for a while. He knew when Harriet went off to have cubs of her own. He thought he would never see her again.

He was wrong.

A **flood** came to the river and the forest. Harriet and her cubs were in danger. Harriet remembered the place where she had been safe as a cub. She took her two cubs one by one across the river to Billy's house.

They stayed there until the floodwaters started to go down.

Harriet watched the river every day. She left her cubs with Billy one day so that she could leave and see her **den**. She decided that her den was safe again. She took the first cub across the river. The flow of the river was strong.

Harriet asked for help with her second cub. She walked down to Billy's boat. She jumped in. Harriet waited for Billy to see her in the boat. He did. Billy knew right away that Harriet was asking for a ride across the river.

Billy rowed Harriet and her cub across the river to the forest. She and her cubs went back to live in the wild again.

Billy still lives on the farm near the forest. He still helps animals. He once said in an interview that Harriet was the love of his life. Her trust in Billy was like a bridge between wild animals and humans.

---

orphan: an animal or person who has no parents
flood: a large amount of water that covers land
den: a hollow space used for a home by a wild animal

The Leopard That Went for Help

Billy Arjan Singh is a wildlife expert. He lives on a farm in India. At his home across the river from a big forest, he takes in **orphans**. These orphans have four legs and whiskers!

Billy works with big cats, like leopards and tigers.

One orphan cub was a leopard named Harriet. From the first day, Billy started to teach Harriet how to go back and live in the wild. He built tree platforms to teach her how to climb. He took her on walks in the forest and showed her how to hunt.

Finally, Harriet learned her lessons about living in the wild. She was ready to go live in the forest. Billy rowed Harriet across the river to the trees where she went into the forest on her own. Billy thought that he would never see her again.

He was wrong.

Floods came to the forest. Harriet and her cubs were in danger. Harriet remembered the place where she had been safe as a cub. She took her two cubs one by one across the river to Billy's house.

They stayed there until the floodwaters started to go down.

Harriet watched the river every day. One day, Harriet swam across the river and went to see her **den**. She decided that her den was safe again. She took the first cub across the river. But, the current in the river was strong and she had trouble swimming.

Harriet asked for help. She took her cub in her mouth. She walked down to Billy's boat. She jumped in. Then, she stood there and waited for Billy to see her in the boat. When he did, he knew right away that Harriet was asking for a ride across the river.

Billy rowed Harriet and her cub across the river to the forest. She and her cubs went back to live in the wild again.

Billy still lives on the farm and he still helps animals. He once said in an **interview** that Harriet was the love of his life. Her trust in Billy was like a bridge between wild animals and humans.

---

orphan: an animal or person who has no parents
den: a hollow space used for a home by a wild animal
interview: a meeting where one person asks another person questions to get
        information

The Leopard That Went for Help

Billy Arjan Singh is a wildlife expert. He lives in India on his farm, which is across a river from a large forest. There, Billy takes in **orphans**—orphans that have four legs and whiskers!

Billy works with leopards and tigers.

One leopard cub that grew up on Billy's farm was named Harriet. From the first day, Billy started to teach Harriet how to go back and live in the wild. He built tree platforms to teach her how to climb. He took her on walks and showed her how to hunt.

Finally, Harriet learned about living in the wild. She was ready to go live in the forest. Billy rowed Harriet across the river where she went into the forest on her own. Billy thought that he would never see her again.

He was wrong.

Floods arrived at the river and the forest. Harriet and her cubs were in danger. Harriet remembered the place where she had been protected as a cub. She took her cubs to Billy's house.

They stayed there until the floodwaters started to go down.

Harriet watched the river every day. One day, Harriet went to check on her **den**. She decided that her den was **secure** again. She took the first cub across the river. The current was strong and she had difficulty swimming.

Harriet knew that if she swam across with the second cub, she would be putting them both in harm's way. So, Harriet the wild leopard asked for help. She took her cub in her mouth, walked down to Billy's boat, and jumped in waiting for Billy to see her. Billy knew right away that Harriet was asking for a ride across the river.

Billy rowed Harriet and her cub safely across the river to the forest where she and her cubs went back to live in the wild again.

Billy still lives on the farm and he still helps animals. He once said in an **interview** that Harriet was the love of his life. Her trust in Billy was like a bridge between wild animals and humans.

> **orphan:** an animal or person who has no parents
> **secure:** safe
> **den:** a hollow space used for a home by a wild animal
> **interview:** information gained from questions asked to a person

The Leopard That Went for Help

Answer the questions.

1. Who was Harriet?

    A. a dog

    B. Billy's sister

    C. Billy's pet

    D. a leopard

2. Why did Billy take Harriet to the forest and leave her there?

    A. He wanted to get rid of her.

    B. He wanted her to live in the wild where she belonged.

    C. He wanted her to live part of the time in the forest.

    D. all of the above

Write **T** for true or **F** for false.

3. _____ A huge forest fire put Harriet and her cubs in danger.

4. _____ Billy Singh lives in the forest.

5. _____ Billy built platforms in the trees to teach Harriet to climb.

6. Why do you think Harriet watched the river every day?

    A. She wanted to take her cubs back to the forest.

    B. She wanted to see if her den was safe again.

    C. She didn't like Billy anymore.

    D. A. and B.

7. How did Harriet ask Billy for help at the end of the story?

    A. She brought her cubs to his farm.

    B. She stood in his boat and waited for him to row across the river.

    C. She lived in his house.

    D. She left her cubs in his care when she went to look at her den.

8. Based on Harriet's actions in the story, what can you infer about her? Write your answer on another sheet of paper.

Stars on Earth

Some people are looking up at hills in West Texas. They see glowing red lights. Are they the headlights of cars on the highway? Are they the lights of campfires? The lights are moving! But, they are not moving the way cars move. The lights go up and down. Then, they disappear!

People go to look at the **famous** Marfa lights. They are named for the town of Marfa, Texas. The lights can be seen when you look at the hills from far away. There have been many ideas about these strange lights over the years. One **theory** is that the lights are the headlights of cars driving down the road.

That could not be true. People in the 1880s wrote about the lights. That was long before there were cars with headlights. People thought the Marfa lights were the campfires of the Apaches. People would ride into the hills. They could not find any campsites or fires. They found out that the Apaches could also see the lights. The Apaches said that the lights were stars that had come down to Earth.

Some people say that the lights are moonlight shining on rocks in the hills. Others say they are made by gas from swamps. Some scientists think that they are light from planets or stars. They say that the lights **reflect** in a strange way on the hills. That does not help explain how the lights move. These dancing lights stay a mystery.

famous: well-known
theory: a thought or belief about a set of facts
reflect: to return light

Stars on Earth

Some people are looking up at a group of low hills in West Texas. Suddenly, they see glowing, reddish-orange lights. Are they the headlights of cars on the highway? Are they the lights of campfires? The people shout and point. The lights are moving! But, they aren't moving the way cars move. They go up in the air. They fall back to the earth. And then...they simply disappear!

Every night, people go to look at the famous Marfa lights. They are named for the town of Marfa, Texas. The lights can be seen east of the town when you look at the hills in the distance. There have been many ideas about these strange lights over the years. One **theory** is that the lights are the headlights of cars driving down the road.

But, that could not be true. Settlers in the 1880s wrote about the lights. That was long before there were cars with headlights. At that time, pioneers thought the Marfa lights were the campfires of Apaches in the hills. When they would ride into the hills, they could not find **evidence** of campsites or fires. Later, the settlers learned that the Apaches, too, could see the lights. They said the lights were stars that had come down to Earth.

Some people say that the lights are moonlight shining on minerals in the hills. Others say they are made by gas from swamps. Some scientists have tried to prove that the lights really are light from planets or stars. They say that the lights **reflect** in a strange way on the hills. That doesn't help us understand why the lights can "dance." They move up and down, slow down, and speed up. These dancing "stars," the Marfa lights, stay a mystery.

theory: thoughts or beliefs about a set of facts
evidence: something that shows proof
reflect: to return light

Stars on Earth

Some people are gazing at a group of low hills in West Texas. Suddenly, they notice glowing reddish-orange lights. Are they the headlights of vehicles on the highway? Are they the lights of campfires? The people shout and point because the lights are moving! But, they aren't moving the way cars move. They shoot up in the air. They fall back to the earth. And then... they simply disappear!

Every night, people go to witness the famous Marfa lights. The lights are named for the town of Marfa, Texas, where these lights can be witnessed in the distant hills east of the town. Over the years there have been many beliefs about these strange lights. One **theory** is that the lights are the headlights of cars driving down the road.

But, that could not be true. Settlers in the 1880s wrote about the lights long before there were cars with headlights. At that time, **pioneers** thought the Marfa lights were the campfires of Apaches in the hills. When the pioneers would ride into the hills, they could find no **evidence** of campsites or fires. Later, the settlers learned that the Apaches, too, could see the lights. They thought the lights were stars that had come down to Earth.

Some people say that the lights are moonlight shining on minerals in the hills. Others say they are made by gases from swamps. Some scientists have tried to prove that lights from planets or stars **reflect** in a strange way on the hills. That doesn't help us understand why the lights "dance." They move up and down, slow down, and speed up. These dancing "stars," the Marfa lights, stay a mystery.

theory: thoughts or beliefs about a set of facts
pioneer: a person who explores a new area
evidence: something that shows proof
reflect: to return light

Stars on Earth

Answer the questions.

Read the following sentence and answer the questions.

And then...they simply disappear!

When added to a word, the prefix *dis-* means the opposite. *Disappear* is the opposite of *appear*. Add *dis-* to the following words and write their meanings.

1. approve _____

2. able _____

3. agree _____

4. obey _____

5. From where did the Marfa lights get their name? Write your answer in a complete sentence.

_____

_____

6. Which of the following is not a feature of the Marfa lights?

    A. They are always blueish white.

    B. They move up and down.

    C. They can speed up and slow down.

    D. B. and C.

Write **T** for true or **F** for false.

7. _____ Early settlers could not see the lights.

8. _____ People saw the lights before cars with headlights were invented.

9. _____ Early settlers thought the lights might be campfires.

10. _____ Some scientists think the lights are from stars or planets.

11. Circle the phrase about the Marfa lights that is not a theory discussed in the story.

    reflected starlight   lights from boats

    moonlight on minerals   stars coming down to Earth

      swamp gas

12. What is your theory about the Marfa lights? On another sheet of paper, write your thoughts about these mysterious lights.

Taking Flight

The Wright brothers made the first working airplane. Or did they? Scientists have made some strange finds. These things show that people thought about building airplanes long ago. Did they end up make these flying machines?

A model of a flying object was found in a **tomb** in Egypt. Explorers found it. They put it in a box marked "wooden bird model." That was in 1898. This was before a working airplane was made. A scientist opened the box years later. The scientist had seen an airplane. He knew the model was not a bird. The model looks just like a glider plane. It was made about 200 BC in Egypt. Builders in Egypt often made small models of things they planned to make.

Another strange thing was found in South America. It is a small, gold model with wings. The people of Colombia made many little gold animals. These gold **trinkets** are found in tombs. This model does not look like a bird. It does not look like a bug. It looks like a little airplane. Was it meant to be a flying machine?

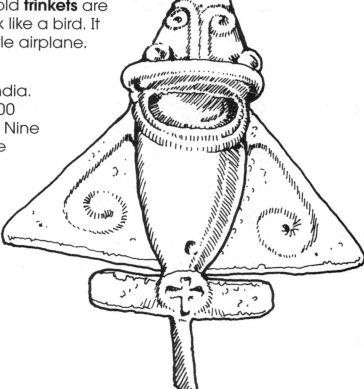

Then, there are **ancient** stories from India. These stories were written more than 2,000 years ago. The authors were called "The Nine Unknown Men." These stories say that the ancient Indians knew how to fly. They had airplanes shaped like circles. These circles had domed tops. They had windows all around them. The stories tell how these machines flew "with the speed of the wind." Is this proof that ancient people built airplanes?

tomb: a place where the dead are buried
trinket: small object; ornament
ancient: existed many years ago; old

Taking Flight

Everyone knows that the Wright brothers made the first working airplane. Or did they? Scientists have made some strange finds. They seem to show that people thought about building airplanes long ago. Did they actually make these flying machines?

A model of a flying object was found in a **tomb** in Egypt. Explorers found it and put it in a box marked "wooden bird model." That was in 1898, before a working airplane was invented. Years later, another scientist opened the box. By then, a working airplane had been invented. The scientist had seen an airplane, so he knew the model was not a bird! The model looks just like a glider plane. It even has curved wings, like the ones on the Concorde jet. This model was made about 200 BC. In Egypt, builders often made small models of things they planned to build. Did they build this airplane?

Another strange thing was found in South America. It is a small, gold model with wings. The people of Colombia made many little gold animals. These gold **trinkets** are found in tombs. But, this model does not look like a bird. It does not look like a bug. It looks like a strange little airplane. Was it meant to be a flying machine?

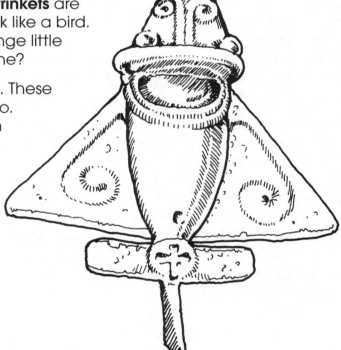

Then, there are **ancient** stories from India. These texts were written more than 2,000 years ago. The authors were called "The Nine Unknown Men." In these writings, it says that the ancient Indians knew how to fly. They had airplanes shaped like circles. These circles had domed ceilings. They had **portholes** all around them. They sound like flying saucers! The stories tell how these machines flew "with the speed of the wind." Is this proof that ancient people built airplanes?

tomb: a place where the dead are buried
trinket: small object; ornament
ancient: existed many years ago; old
porthole: round window usually found on ships and submarines

Taking Flight

Everyone knows that the Wright brothers made the first working airplane. Or did they? Scientists have made some extraordinary finds. These finds seem to illustrate that people thought about building airplanes long ago. Did they actually make these flying machines?

A model of a flying object was found in a tomb in Egypt. Explorers found it and placed it in a box marked "wooden bird model." That was in 1898, before a working airplane was invented. Years later, another scientist opened the box. By then, a working airplane had been invented. The scientist had seen an airplane, so he knew the model was not a bird. The model looks just like a glider plane. It even has curved wings, like the ones on the Concorde jet. This model was made about 200 BC. In Egypt, builders often made small models of things they planned to build. Did they build this airplane?

Another strange thing was found in South America. It is a small, gold model with wings. The people of Colombia made many miniature gold animals. These gold **trinkets** are found in **tombs**. But, this model does not look like a bird. It does not look like a bug. It looks like a strange little airplane. Was it meant to be a flying machine?

Then, there are **ancient** writings from India. These texts were written more than 2,000 years ago. The authors were called "The Nine Unknown Men." In these writings, it says that the ancient Indians knew how to fly. They had airplanes shaped like circles. These circles had domed ceilings. They had **portholes** all around them. They sound like flying saucers! The writings tell how these machines flew "with the speed of the wind." Is this evidence that ancient people invented airplanes?

trinkets: small objects; ornaments
tomb: a place where the dead are buried
ancient: existed many years ago; old
porthole: round window usually found on ships and submarines

Taking Flight

Answer the questions.

1. Which of the following sentences does not contain two adjectives?

    A. It looks like a strange little airplane.

    B. Explorers found a wooden bird model in a tomb.

    C. The model looks just like a glider plane.

    D. It was a small gold model with wings.

2. Read about the flying machine in the stories from India. How is that flying machine different from an airplane today? Write your answer in a complete sentence.

    _____

3. Why did the explorers who found the wooden model think it looked like a bird and not an airplane?

    A. In 1898, airplanes looked different.

    B. The explorers didn't look at it carefully.

    C. In 1898, few people knew what an airplane was.

    D. The explorers had bad eyesight.

4. The word *tomb* in the story has a silent *b*. Circle the words that are spelled with a silent letter.

    plumber   knife   graph   island   debt

    wrap   climb   hoe   castle

5. Which of the following is not talked about in the story?

    A. a small, gold airplane from Colombia

    B. a model found in a tomb in Egypt

    C. drawings of airplanes by Leonardo da Vinci

    D. ancient Indian stories about flying machines

6. Findings of early flying machines were made in which three places?

    A. Russia, India, and Egypt

    B. India, Egypt, and Canada

    C. Egypt, Colombia, and India

    D. Colombia, Europe, and India

7. Do you think ancient people built flying machines? Why or why not? Write your answer on another sheet of paper.

Faster Than a Speeding Bullet

Can a train ride be as fast as a plane ride? It can if you are rocketing along in a bullet train. This is a great form of train travel. It is getting more **popular** every day.

Bullet trains were first used in Japan. The trains were made in 1957. They started running in 1959. It used to take seven hours to go from one end of Japan to the other on a train. The same ride on the bullet train took about three and a half hours. The first bullet train was the fastest train in the world.

But, even that first bullet train would look slow today! Today, most bullet trains can run between 200 and 300 miles per hour (321.87 and 482.8 kmh). Newer trains can be even faster.

Japan is not the only country with these trains. Many places in Europe have bullet trains too. It is now faster to take the train than it is to fly in a plane.

There are three things that help these trains go fast. One is the shape of the train. It has a long, flat nose in front. It has low cars. This **improves** the wind flow over the train. The wind does not slow the train down. Another thing that helps are tracks with no sharp curves. All of the curves are long and smooth. The train does not have to slow down as it travels. Finally, the tracks never cross roads or other tracks. The train never has to stop for other traffic.

What does it feel like to be on a bullet train? The speed is so fast the land is a **blur**. Most people say it feels more like flying in a plane than being on the ground.

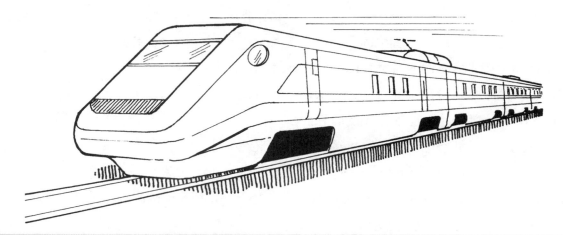

popular: common to most people
improve: to make better; helps
blur: something moving too quickly to see

Faster Than a Speeding Bullet

Can a train ride be as fast as a plane ride? It can if you are rocketing along in a bullet train. This is an extreme form of train travel. It is getting more **popular** every day.

Bullet trains were first used in Japan. The trains were planned in 1957. They started running in 1959. Before the bullet train, it took seven hours to go from one end of Japan to the other. The same ride on the bullet train took about three and a half hours. When the first bullet train started to run, it was the fastest train in the world.

But, even that first bullet train would look slow today! Today, most bullet trains can run between 200 and 300 miles per hour (321.87 and 482.8 kmh). Newer models can be even faster.

Japan is not the only country with these super trains. Many countries in Europe have them too. In many of these countries, it is now faster to take the train than it is to fly in a plane.

How do bullet trains go so fast? There are three things that help these trains speed along. One is the shape of the train. It is shaped with a long, flat nose in front and has low cars. This **improves** the wind flow over the train. The wind does not slow the train down. Another thing that helps are tracks with no sharp curves. All of the curves are long and smooth so that the train does not have to slow down as it travels. Finally, the special bullet-train tracks never cross roads or other train tracks. The train never has to stop for other traffic.

What does it feel like to be on a bullet train? The speed is so fast that you cannot see anything outside the windows. The land is a **blur**. Most people say it feels more like flying in a plane than being on the ground.

popular: common to most people
improve: to make better; help
blur: something moving too quickly to see

3.RI.4, 3.RI.5, 3.RI.10, 3.RF.4, 3.L.4

Faster Than a Speeding Bullet

Can a train ride be as fast as a plane ride? It can if you are rocketing along in a bullet train. This is an extreme form of train travel. It is getting more **popular** every day.

Bullet trains were first used in Japan. The trains were designed in 1957 and started running in 1959. Before the bullet train, it took seven hours to go from one end of Japan to the other. The same ride on the bullet train took about three and a half hours. When the first bullet train started to run, it was the fastest train in the world.

But, even that first bullet train would look slow today! Today, most bullet trains can run between 200 and 300 miles per hour (321.87 and 482.8 kmh). Newer models can be even faster.

Japan is not the only country with these super trains. Many countries in Europe have them, too. In many of these countries, it is now faster to take the train than it is to fly in an airplane.

How do bullet trains go so fast? There are three things that help these trains speed along. First is the shape of the train. It is shaped with a long, flat nose in front and has low cars. This helps reduce **air resistance** on the train. The wind does not slow down the train. Another thing that helps the bullet train travel rapidly is tracks with no sharp curves. All of the curves are long and smooth so that the train does not have to brake as it travels. Finally, the special bullet-train tracks never cross roads or other train tracks. The train never has to stop for other traffic.

What does it feel like to be on a bullet train? The speed is so fast that you cannot see anything outside the windows. The land is a **blur**. Most people say it feels more like flying in an airplane than traveling close to the ground.

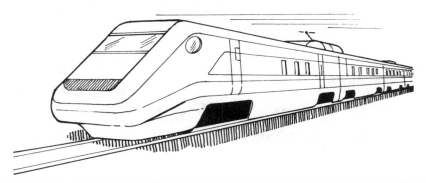

popular: common to most people
air resistance: force put on an object by air
blur: something moving too quickly to see

3.RI.1, 3.RI.4, 3.RI.7, 3.W.1, 3.L.4

Faster Than a Speeding Bullet

Answer the questions.

Complete each sentence.

1. The first bullet train was in the country of _____.

2. Today, there are many bullet trains in _____, as well as Asia.

3. Traveling in a bullet train feels more like being in a _____ than a train.

4. The first bullet train started running in the year _____.

Write **T** for true or **F** for false.

5. _____ One reason the bullet train can go so fast is that it has low cars.

6. _____ The nose of a bullet train is high and peaked.

7. _____ When you ride in a bullet train, the land outside can be a blur.

8. _____ The first bullet train was twice as fast as an old-fashioned train.

9. Read the following sentences from the story and answer the question.

   Can a train ride be as fast as a plane ride? It can if you are rocketing along in a bullet train.

   Which of the following is a word that could replace *rocketing*?

   A. speeding

   B. racing

   C. wandering

   D. A. and B.

10. Would you like to ride on a bullet train? Why or why not? Write your answer on another sheet of paper.

A World of Robots

People have told stories about robots for many years. They told about machines that can help us live better lives. You can see such robots in movies.

The first movie robot was shown in a 1924 film. The movie showed robots doing boring tasks. Is a world of robots just a dream?

Robots are now a part of real life. Robots have only been around for about 50 years. First, scientists had to make a "brain" for robots. People made the computer chip. Many robots have **sensors**. Sensors help robots "see" light. Sensors help robots "feel" things around them. People give **commands** to robots. The sensors tell the robot to move in one way or another. Now, a robot can do a job. What kinds of jobs do robots do?

Just like in the 1924 movie, robots today can do things over and over again without getting **fatigued**. They paint things. They make car parts. They put food in boxes. They build computer chips too!

Robots also have dangerous jobs. People use robots to take apart bombs. Robots can crawl into water pipes to see if they are clogged. Scientists built a robot that can walk into a volcano to get rock samples.

And, robots have gone places where people cannot. The Mars rover is a robot that works on Mars. What other jobs could robots do in the future?

We will have robots that will be able to learn new things. These robots will know that a book cannot break, but an egg can.

They will be able to talk and listen to people. They will know when people are happy or sad. They will be able to do chores. Our lives may become more like the movies of the past.

sensor: something that responds to light and sound
command: an order given
fatigued: tired

A World of Robots

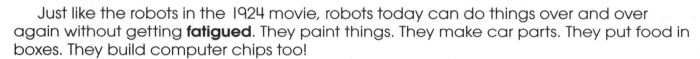

People have told stories about robots for many years. They told about machines that can help us live better lives. You can see such robots in movies.

The first movie robot was shown in a 1924 film. In the movie, robots were made to do the tasks people thought were boring. Is a world of robots just a dream?

Robots are now a part of real life. But, robots have only been around for about 50 years. First, scientists had to create a type of "brain" for robots. That happened when people made computer chips. Many robots also have **sensors** inside them. These help robots "see" light and "feel" walls or things in their paths. Sensors also help people give **commands** to robots. A robot can be told to move in one way or another. By following these movements, a robot can do a job. What kinds of jobs do people give to robots?

Just like the robots in the 1924 movie, robots today can do things over and over again without getting **fatigued**. They paint things. They make car parts. They put food in boxes. They build computer chips too!

Robots also have jobs that are dangerous. People use robots to take apart bombs. Robots can crawl into pipes to see if something is blocking water flow. Scientists have even built a robot that can walk into a volcano to get rock samples.

And, robots have gone places where humans cannot. The Mars rover is a robot that works on Mars. What other jobs could robots do in the future?

In the future, we will have robots that know how to handle objects around them. These robots will know that a book cannot break, but an egg can. They will be able to learn new things.

They will be able to talk and listen to people. They will know when people are happy or sad. They will be able to cook, talk on the phone, and write. Our lives may become more and more like the movies of the past.

sensor: something that responds to light and sound
command: an order given
fatigued: tired

A World of Robots

For many years, people have told stories about robots that can perform the jobs of humans. These machines can help us live better lives. You can see such robots in movies.

The first movie robot was shown in a film made in 1924. In the movie, robots were made to free humans from **mundane** tasks. Sometimes, they act like friends. Is a world of robots just a dream?

Robots are now a part of real life. However, robots have only been around for about 50 years. Before robots could be made, scientists had to invent a type of "brain" for them. That happened when people created computer chips. Many robots also have sensors inside them. The **sensors** help robots "see" light and "feel" walls or things in their paths. Sensors also help by recognizing **commands** given to robots by people. Commands tell a robot to move in one way or another. By moving in these ways, a robot can do a specific job. What kinds of jobs do people give to robots?

Just like the robots in the 1924 movie, robots today can do repetitive tasks without getting **fatigued**. They paint things, make car parts, place food in boxes, and even build computer chips too!

Robots are programmed to do jobs that are dangerous for people. Robots can take apart bombs. Robots can crawl into pipes to see if something is blocking the flow of water. Scientists have even built a robot that can enter into a volcano to collect rock samples.

And, robots have helped explore deep underwater places and very cold places where humans cannot go. The Mars rover is a robot that works on the planet Mars. What other jobs could people give to robots in the future?

In the future, we will have robots that know how to handle different objects around them. These robots will know that a book cannot break easily, but an egg can. They will be able to learn new things.

They will be able to communicate with people. They will recognize human emotions. They will be able to cook, talk on the phone, and write. With robots like these, our lives may become more and more like the science fiction movies of the past.

mundane: boring; repetitive
sensor: something that responds to light and sound
command: an order given
fatigued: tired

A World of Robots

Answer the questions.

1. What helps a robot "see" or "feel" things?

> **A.** samples
>
> **B.** dreams
>
> **C.** sensors
>
> **D.** fingers

Write **T** for true or **F** for false.

2. _____ Robots can get tired doing their jobs.

3. _____ Scientists made a robot that walks into volcanoes.

4. _____ Robots have computer chips that work like brains.

5. List three things that robots may be able to do in the future.

_____

_____

_____

6. Circle the verbs.

paint	robot	learn
real	build	crawl
task	movie	walk

7. Choose two words from the vocabulary box under your story. Use them each in a sentence.

_____

_____

8. Explain how your life might change if you had a robot. Write your answer on another sheet of paper.

To the Stars

In Coalwood, West Virginia, many young men became miners. That's what Homer Hickam could have done too. Mining was hard work. Sometimes, there was great danger. Homer's own father wanted him to work for the mine. That was before the **rockets**.

In 1957, Homer was 14 years old. Russian scientists had **launched** the first **satellite**, called *Sputnik,* into space. Homer watched it streak through the sky. That is when Homer decided to make a rocket. He and five friends built one together. It blew up Homer's fence!

Homer did not give up. Homer started to read. His teacher, Miss Riley, gave him a book. Homer needed to learn some hard math to be able to read the book. He did it. Homer and his friends built 11 more rockets. All of them failed. People in town started calling them "The Rocket Boys."

The Rocket Boys learned all they could about math and science. They changed the way that they built the rockets. The boys put everything that they learned into a science project. They won a national medal for their work.

By 1960, The Rocket Boys had built 31 rockets. The last one was over five feet (1.52 m) tall. People in town came to watch the rocket go into the air. It was the last rocket that Homer built in Coalwood. The rockets had changed his life. He ended up working for NASA. His dreams took him to the stars.

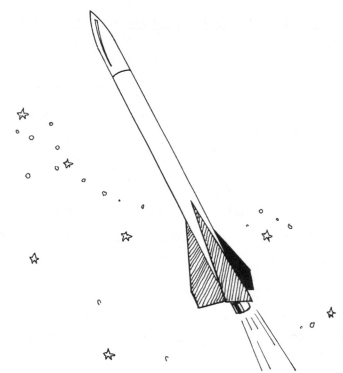

rocket: object pushed into the air by gases
launch: to send into the air
satellite: an object that orbits Earth or other body in space

To the Stars

In Coalwood, West Virginia, many boys became miners when they grew up. That's what Homer Hickam could have done too. The mine owners owned the entire town of Coalwood. Mining was hard work. Sometimes, there was great danger. But, it was all that the town knew how to do. Homer's own father wanted him to work for the mine. That was before the **rockets**.

In 1957, Homer was 14 years old. Russian scientists had **launched** the first **satellite**, called *Sputnik*, into space. While standing with the other people of his town, Homer watched it streak through the sky. That's when Homer decided to build his own rocket. He and five friends built one together. It blew up the fence outside of Homer's house!

Instead of giving up, Homer started to read. His teacher, Miss Riley, gave him a book. In order to understand it, Homer learned some hard math. Homer and his friends helped each other. They built 11 more rockets. All of them failed. People in town started calling them "The Rocket Boys."

The Rocket Boys learned everything they could about math and science. They changed the way that they built the rockets. Then, they put everything that they learned into a science fair project. They won a national gold medal for their work.

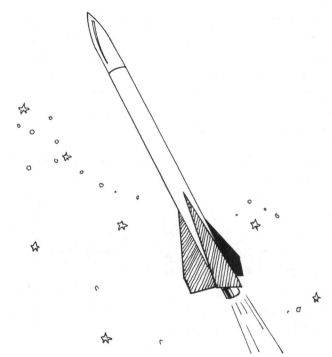

By 1960, The Rocket Boys had built 31 rockets. The last one was over five feet (1.52 m) tall. Almost everyone in the town came to watch the rocket go into the air. It was the last rocket that Homer built in Coalwood. But, the rockets had changed his life. He ended up working for the United States government at NASA instead of in the coal mine. His dreams took him to the stars.

rocket: object pushed into the air by gases
launch: to send into the air
satellite: an object that orbits Earth or other body in space

To the Stars

In Coalwood, West Virginia, many boys became miners when they grew up. That's what Homer Hickam could have done too. The mine owners owned the entire town of Coalwood. Mining was hard work. Sometimes, there was great danger. But, it was all that the town knew how to do. Homer's own father wanted him to work for the mine. That was before the **rockets**.

In 1957, Homer was 14 years old. Russian scientists had **launched** the first **satellite**, called *Sputnik*, into space. While standing with some other people from his town, Homer watched it streak through the sky. That is when Homer decided to build his own rocket. He and five friends built one together. It blew up the fence outside of Homer's house!

Instead of giving up, Homer started to read about rockets. His teacher, Miss Riley, gave him a book. In order to understand it, Homer needed to learn some challenging math. He eventually did it. Homer and his friends helped each other. They built 11 more rockets, and all of them failed. People in town started calling them "The Rocket Boys."

The Rocket Boys educated themselves in math and science that would help them build better rockets. They changed the way that they built the rockets. Then, they put everything that they learned into a science fair project. The boys won a national gold medal for their work.

By 1960, The Rocket Boys had built 31 rockets. The last one was over five feet (1.52 m) tall. Almost everyone in the town came to watch the rocket launch into the air. It was the last rocket that Homer built in Coalwood. However, the rockets had changed his life. Instead of working in the coal mine like his father, Homer ended up working for the United States government at NASA. One could say that his dreams took him to the stars.

rocket: object pushed into the air by gases
launch: to send into the air
satellite: an object that orbits Earth or other body in space

To the Stars

Answer the questions.

1. What did Homer Hickam decide to do when he was 14?

   A. He wanted to build a satellite.   **B.** He decided to blow up a fence.

   C. He wanted to fly in a *Sputnik*.   **D.** none of the above

2. Read the following sentence from the story and answer the question.

   While standing with the other people of his town, Homer watched it streak through the sky.

   What is another word for *streak*?

   A. stream   **B.** stretch

   C. race   **D.** wander

3. In order to build his rockets, Homer had to do all of the following except

   A. learn how to fly.   **B.** learn more science.

   C. learn difficult math.   **D.** get help from his friends.

4. Which sentence shows correct capitalization?

   A. Russian Scientists had launched the first satellite, called *sputnik*, into space.

   B. Russian scientists had launched the first satellite, called *Sputnik*, into space.

   C. russian scientists had launched the first Satellite, called *sputnik*, into space.

   D. Russian Scientists had launched the first Satellite, called *sputnik*, into space.

5. Homer and his friends won a gold medal at _____.

   A. NASA.   **B.** a local science fair.

   C. Coalwood.   **D.** a national science fair.

6. Write the missing verbs.

Past	Present	Future
_____	build	will build
launched	launch	_____
flew	_____	will fly

7. How did the rockets change Homer's life? Write your answer on another sheet of paper.

Olympic Spirit

Wilma Rudolph did not give up. She only weighed four and a half pounds (2.04 kg) when she was born. Wilma was sick many times when she was young. Her family was poor. They could not pay for a doctor. Her mother took care of her. One time, Wilma got **pneumonia**. After she got better, Wilma's parents saw that one of her legs was weak.

This time, Wilma's family had to pay for a doctor. The news was bad. Wilma had **polio**. Today, there are shots that keep people from getting polio. But, Wilma was born in 1940 before a **vaccine** was made.

The doctor said that Wilma would never walk again. The doctor put braces on her legs. Wilma was always trying to take them off. Her brothers and sisters made sure she kept the braces on. It was very hard work to make her legs strong. Wilma was 11 years old when she took off her braces forever.

What did Wilma want to do after taking off her braces? She wanted to play sports! She started playing basketball. Three years passed before her coach would let her play. When he finally did, Wilma set a state record. That was only the start!

Wilma was a great track star. She won three gold medals in the 1960 Olympics. She was the first woman to do that. It was a long trip from being a sick child to winning medals at the Olympics. Wilma Rudolph made it because she did not give up.

pneumonia: a disease where lungs fill with fluid
polio: a disease that can disable muscles
vaccine: a shot that protects against a disease

Olympic Spirit

Wilma Rudolph did not give up. She was a small and sickly child. She weighed four and a half pounds (2.04 kg) when she was born. Wilma was sick a lot when she was young. Her family was poor. They could not pay for a doctor. Her mother took care of her. Things became serious. Wilma got **pneumonia**. After she got better, Wilma's parents saw that one of her legs was weak.

This time, Wilma's family had to pay for a doctor. Wilma had **polio**. Polio is an illness that can make legs or arms hard to use. Today, there are shots that keep people from getting polio. But, Wilma was born in 1940 before a **vaccine** was made.

The doctor said that Wilma would never walk again. The doctor put braces on her legs. Wilma was always trying to take them off. Her brothers and sisters made sure she kept the braces on. Wilma went to the hospital once a week. It was very hard work to make her legs strong. Wilma took off her braces forever when she was 11 years old.

What did Wilma want to do after taking off her braces? She wanted to play sports! She started playing basketball. Three years passed before her coach would let her play. When he finally did, Wilma set a state record. That was only the beginning!

Wilma Rudolph went on to become a great track star. She won three gold medals in the 1960 Olympics. She was the first woman to do that. It was a long trip from her sickness-filled childhood to the Olympics. Wilma Rudolph made it because she did not give up.

---

pneumonia: a disease where lungs fill with fluid
polio: a disease that can disable muscles
vaccine: a shot that protects against a disease

Olympic Spirit

It would have been very easy for Wilma Rudolph to give up. She was a small and sickly child. She only weighed four and a half pounds (2.04 kg) when she was born. In the first years of her life, Wilma's mother helped her when she had the measles, the mumps, chicken pox, and scarlet fever because the family could not afford a doctor. Then, things became even more serious. Wilma got **pneumonia**. After she beat pneumonia, Wilma's parents saw that one of her legs was weak.

The Rudolph family was very poor. This time, they had to pay for a doctor. The news was not good. Wilma had **polio**. Today, there are shots that protect people from polio. But, Wilma was born in 1940 before a **vaccine** was created.

The doctor told Wilma's parents that she would never walk. Wilma had a different idea. The doctor put braces on her legs. Wilma said that she was always trying to take them off. Wilma's brothers and sisters watched her to make sure she kept the braces on. They helped rub her legs to make them better. Wilma also went to the hospital once a week. It was very hard work to make her legs strong. But, Wilma was brave. When she was 11 years old, Wilma took off her braces forever.

What did Wilma want to do after spending her whole life barely able to walk? She wanted to play sports! She started by playing basketball. Even after she joined a team, three years passed before her coach would let her play. Wilma did not give up. When her coach finally let her play, she set a state record. That was only the beginning! Wilma Rudolph went on to become a great track star. She won three gold medals in the 1960 Olympics. She was the first woman to do that. It was a long trip from her sickness-filled childhood to the Olympics. Wilma Rudolph made it because of her **courageous** spirit.

pneumonia: a disease where lungs fill with fluid
polio: a disease that can disable muscles
vaccine: an injection that protects against a disease
courageous: brave

Olympic Spirit

Answer the questions.

1. Wilma Rudolph became

    A. a famous Olympian.   **B.** a famous baseball player.

    C. the first woman to fly.   **D.** a famous politician.

Write **T** for true and **F** for false.

2. _____ Wilma won three gold medals in basketball.

3. _____ Wilma's family was poor and they could not afford a doctor.

4. _____ Wilma was scared to take off her braces.

5. Read the following sentence from the story and answer the question.

The doctor put braces on her legs.

Which of the following definitions of *braces* is used in this sentence?

    A. clasps that hold things together

    B. suspenders

    C. metal supports for the body

    D. plant firmly

6. Circle three adjectives that tell about Wilma Rudolph as a child.

        fast   poor   sickly

        healthy   angry   small

7. What is *track*?

    A. a sporting event that features passing a ball

    B. a game like hockey

    C. sporting events that feature running

    D. none of the above

8. Write two sentences that tell how Wilma's family helped her.

_____

_____

9. Do you think that Wilma Rudolph would have accomplished the same things if she had not been sick as a child? Why or why not? Write your answer on another sheet of paper.

The Violin as a Voice

Sarah Chang says that the violin is the closest music to the human voice. She has been hearing that voice most of her life. Sarah was only three years old when she got a violin. Her parents helped her learn to play. Sarah was very good. She was five when she went to a famous music school called Juilliard.

Sarah's father was her first teacher. He also plays violin. Her mother is a **composer**. She helped Sarah learn to read music. Sarah has a gift for playing. It has been with her all of her life.

Sarah started to play with **orchestras** when she was eight years old. She had recorded some of her music on CDs by the time she was nine. People love to hear her play. A **famous** musician named Yehudi Menuhin said that Sarah was the most perfect violinist he had ever heard.

Sarah also speaks three languages. She speaks Korean, German, and English. Sarah travels a lot to play with different groups. She says that her whole life is planned. She knows where she will be in two years. She knows what hotel she will be staying in. She knows what she will be practicing on her violin. Sometimes, she does not like that. She wishes that she had more free time. She says if she does not touch a violin for a few days, she misses playing. She also says she loves to play music for other people. That is the most important thing in life for her.

composer: someone who writes music
orchestra: group of people who play music on stringed instruments
famous: well-known

The Violin as a Voice

Sarah Chang says that the violin is the closest music to the human voice. She has been hearing that voice most of her life. Sarah was three years old when she learned how to play violin. Her parents helped her learn to play. Sarah was five years old when she was accepted into a famous music school called Juilliard. Her parents were amazed.

Sarah's father was her first teacher. He also plays violin. Sarah's mother is a **composer**. She helped Sarah learn how to read music. Sarah's gift for playing has been with her all of her life.

Sarah's whole life has been about her talent. She started to play with **orchestras** when she was eight years old. At nine, she had recorded some of her music on CDs. A **famous** musician named Yehudi Menuhin said that Sarah was the most perfect violinist he had ever heard.

Sarah also speaks three languages. She speaks Korean because her parents are from Korea. She also speaks German and English. Sarah travels often to play with different orchestras. She says that her entire life is planned. Sometimes, she doesn't like that. She wishes that she had more free time. She says that if she doesn't touch a violin for a few days, her fingers start to miss playing. She also says she loves to be on the stage playing music for other people. For her, that's the most important thing in life.

composer: someone who writes music
orchestra: group of people who play music on stringed instruments
famous: well-known

The Violin as a Voice

Sarah Chang says that the violin is the closest music to the human voice. She has been hearing that voice most of her life. Sarah was only three years old when she begged her parents for a violin. She learned how to play it right away. Her parents, both musicians, helped her. But, even they were amazed when she was accepted into a famous music school called Juilliard when she was only five years old!

Sarah's father was her first teacher. He also plays violin. Her mother is a **composer**. She helped Sarah learn about reading and understanding music. Sarah's gift for playing, though, seems to have been with her all of her life.

Sarah's entire life has been wrapped up in her musical **talent**. She started to play with **orchestras** when she was eight years old. By the time she was nine, she had recorded some of her music on CDs. People love to hear her play. A **famous** musician named Yehudi Menuhin said that Sarah was the most perfect violinist he had ever heard.

Sarah also speaks three languages. She speaks Korean because her parents are from Korea. She also speaks German and English. Sarah travels often to play with different orchestras. She says that her entire life is planned. If you ask her where she will be two years from now, she knows what hotel she will be staying in and what she will be practicing on her violin. Sometimes, she doesn't like that. She wishes that she had more free time. But, she says if she doesn't touch a violin for three or four days, her fingers start to miss playing. She also says she loves to be on the stage playing music for other people. For her, that's the most important thing in life.

composer: someone who writes music
talent: a special ability
orchestra: group of people who play music on stringed instruments
famous: well-known

The Violin as a Voice

Answer the questions.

Write **T** for true and **F** for false.

1. _____ Yehudi Menuhin is a famous musician.

2. _____ Sarah Chang rarely travels to play her music.

3. _____ Sarah does not like to stop playing violin for more than a few days.

4. _____ Sarah's mother is a doctor.

5. How much time passed between when Sarah got her first violin and when she started school at Juilliard?

    A. 6 months   **B.** I year   **C.** 12 months   **D.** 2 years

6. Which sentence is correct?

    A. Sarah wish that she had more free time.

    B. Sarah wishes that she had more free time.

    C. Sarah wishes that her had more free time.

    D. Sarah wish that she have more free time.

7. Which of the following is not mentioned in the story?

    A. Sarah's birth date   **B.** Sarah's parents and their jobs

    C. Sarah's age when she started playing her violin with orchestras   **D.** the languages that Sarah speaks

8. In the text, you learn that Sarah's mother is a composer. A composer is one who composes. The suffix *-er* is added to *compose*. Write the following words and their meanings.

teach + -er = _____

write + -er = _____

lead + -er = _____

paint + -er = _____

rule + -er = _____

bake + -er = _____

9. Do you think you would like to have a life like Sarah's? Why or why not? Write your answer on another sheet of paper.

Speaking for Animals

Henry Bergh was a rich man. He lived in New York, New York. In 1863, he was asked to go to the royal court of the **czar** of Russia. Henry saw animals treated badly. He did not like it. He wanted to help.

Henry went to London, England, in 1840. He wanted to learn about a group there. This group helped animals. The group was called the Royal Society for the **Prevention** of Cruelty to Animals (RSPCA). This group also helped pass laws. The laws keep animals safe. Henry wanted to start a group like this.

Henry went home in 1866. He held a meeting in New York City. He talked about the goodness and kindness of animals. He said there were no laws to keep animals safe. He told about animals working hard all day. He told about dogs and cats that were not being fed. He told about pets being stolen for money. Henry said that animals could not speak for themselves. That meant that people had to speak for them.

The people agreed. People joined the American Society for the Prevention of Cruelty to Animals (ASPCA). The group was **founded** on April 10, 1866. Nine days later, the city passed laws to help keep animals safe. Henry spent all of his time helping animals. He jumped in if he saw an animal being hurt. When Henry saw a man beating a horse, he took away the whip. Henry would arrest the person himself if he could not find a police officer. Today, the ASPCA still works to help animals around the United States.

czar: a ruler of Russia until 1917
prevention: the act of keeping something from happening
founded: started

Speaking for Animals

Henry Bergh lived in New York, New York. In 1863, he was asked to go to the royal court of the **czar** of Russia. He was asked to **represent** the United States. At the royal court, Henry first saw how badly animals were treated. He did not like it. He wanted to help.

Henry went to London, England, to learn about a group there. In 1840, the British started the Royal Society for the **Prevention** of Cruelty to Animals (RSPCA). This group helped pass laws to keep animals safe. Henry wanted to start a group like this in New York.

Henry went home in 1866. He held a meeting at Clinton Hall in New York City. He talked about the goodness and kindness of animals. He talked about how there were no laws in the United States to keep animals safe. He talked about horses that had to pull heavy carts all day long. He talked about dogs that had to run on treadmills to make machines work. He said that some people just let out their pets at night to find food in garbage cans. Dogcatchers were paid by the number of dogs they caught. Sometimes, they stole pets to get more money. Henry explained that none of these animals could speak for themselves. That meant that people had to speak for them.

People started signing up to join the American Society for the Prevention of Cruelty to Animals (ASPCA) that night. The group was **established** on April 10, 1866. The city passed laws to protect animals nine days later. A few days after the laws passed, Henry saw a man beating a horse with a whip. Henry took away the whip and told the man that he was breaking the law. From that day on, Henry spent all of his time helping animals. If he saw an animal being hurt, he jumped in. If he could not find a police officer, Henry would arrest the person himself! Today, the ASPCA still works to help animals around the United States.

czar: a ruler of Russia until 1917
represent: to serve as an example of
prevention: the act of keeping something from happening
established: formed

Speaking for Animals

Henry Bergh lived in New York, New York. In 1863, he was invited to the royal court of the **czar** of Russia where he was asked to **represent** the United States. At the royal court, Henry first observed how badly animals were treated. He did not like it. He wanted to help.

Henry went to London, England, to learn about a group there. In 1840, the British started the Royal Society for the **Prevention** of Cruelty to Animals (RSPCA). This group helped pass laws to protect animals. Henry wanted to start a group like this in New York.

Henry went home in 1866 where he held a large meeting at Clinton Hall in New York City. He talked to the people about the goodness and kindness of animals. He talked about how there were no laws in the United States to keep people from hurting animals. He told stories about horses that had to pull heavy carts all day long. He talked about dogs that had to run on treadmills to operate machines. He said that some people just let their pets out at night to find food in garbage cans. Dogcatchers at that time were paid by the number of dogs they caught. Sometimes, they stole pets to receive more money. Henry explained that none of these animals could speak for themselves and that meant that people had to speak for them.

People started signing up to join the American Society for the Prevention of Cruelty to Animals (ASPCA) that night. The group was **established** on April 10, 1866. Nine days later, the city passed laws to protect animals. A few days after the laws passed, Henry saw a man beating a horse with a whip. Henry took away the whip. He told the man that he was breaking the law. From that day on, Henry spent all of his time helping animals. Whenever he saw an animal being hurt, he jumped in. If he could not find a police officer, Henry would arrest the person himself! Today, the ASPCA still works to help animals around the United States.

czar: a ruler of Russia until 1917
represent: to serve as an example of
prevention: the act of keeping something from happening
established: formed

Speaking for Animals

Answer the questions.

1. Which of the following animals is not mentioned in the story?

   A. dog

   B. cat

   C. rooster

   D. horse

2. Why did Henry Bergh travel to London?

   A. He was a visitor in the court of the king.

   B. He wanted to see if animals were treated badly there too.

   C. He wanted to go on a vacation before he went home.

   D. He wanted to learn about a group that protected animals.

3. Read the following sentence.

   He talked about the goodness and kindness of animals.

   When the suffix *-ness* is added to the words *good* and *kind,* it changes their parts of speech. Change the following adjectives into nouns by adding the suffix *-ness*. Write their meanings.

   happy _____

   dark _____

   lonely _____

   ill _____

Complete the sentences.

4. The RSPCA was started in the year _____.

5. In the United States in the early 1800s, there were no _____ to keep animals safe.

6. It took _____ for New York City to pass laws to help animals after the ASPCA was formed.

7. Do you think that it is important to protect animals from being treated badly? Why or why not? Write your answer on another sheet of paper. Ask a teacher or classmate to read your essay. Then, revise and rewrite your essay.

Balancing Act

A little boy went to the circus. It was the year 1829. He was five years old. He liked the horses. He liked the clowns. He saw a tightrope walker. He knew that that was what he wanted to do. At home, he put a rope between two chairs. He started to practice. This little boy later took the **stage name** of Charles Blondin.

Charles's father sent him to a school for gymnasts. Then, his father passed away. Charles joined a circus. He was only nine years old. This is how he made his living. When he grew up, he went to the United States. He saw Niagara Falls. Charles knew that he wanted to cross the falls on a tightrope.

The day came for Charles to cross the falls. It was June 30, 1859. A rope that was three inches (7.62 cm) thick was hung across the falls. It was 1,100 feet (335.28 m) long! It sagged more than 100 feet (30.48 m) in the middle. Many people came to watch this **feat**. No one had ever tried it before.

Charles made it across. He wanted to do more. He made more trips across Niagara Falls. Charles had new tricks to please the people. He stood on a chair. He pushed a wheelbarrow across the rope. Charles even walked blindfolded across the tightrope. On one of his most amazing trips, he cooked some eggs on a small stove. Then, he ate them!

All of his trips across Niagara Falls made Charles famous. Later, he performed around Europe. He did not **retire** until he was 68 years old.

stage name: a fake name used by a performer
feat: an act of skill
retire: to end one's career

Balancing Act

A little French boy went to the circus for the first time in 1829. He was five years old. He liked the horses and the clowns. Then, he saw a tightrope walker. He knew that was what he wanted to do. This little boy later took the **stage name** of Charles Blondin.

Charles's father sent him to a school for gymnasts. After his father passed away, Charles joined a circus to make his living. He was only nine years old. When he grew up, he went to the United States. On that trip, he saw Niagara Falls. It was just like the time when he first saw the tightrope walker. Charles knew that he had to cross the falls on a tightrope.

The great day was June 30, 1859. Charles's team put up a rope that was three inches (7.62 cm) thick and 1,100 feet (335.28 m) long. The rope sagged in the middle. It was close to 300 feet (91.44 m) above the falls! Many people came to watch this **feat**. No one had ever tried it before.

Charles made it across safely. He wanted to do more. He made more trips across Niagara Falls. Charles had new tricks to please the people. One time, he stood on a chair. Another time, he pushed a wheelbarrow across the rope. Charles even walked across the tightrope blindfolded. On one of his most amazing trips, he cooked some eggs on a small stove. Then, he ate them!

His trips across Niagara Falls made Charles famous. Later, he performed around Europe. He did not **retire** until he was 68 years old.

---

stage name: a fake name used by a performer
feat: an act of skill
retire: to end one's career

Balancing Act

A little French boy went to the circus for the first time in 1829. He was five years old. He liked the horses and the clowns. Then, he saw a tightrope walker. He knew that that was what he wanted to do. As soon as he was home, he stretched a rope between two chairs and started to practice. This little boy later took the **stage name** of Charles Blondin.

Charles's father sent his son to a special school for gymnasts. When his father died, Charles joined a circus to make his living. He was only nine years old. When he grew up, Charles joined a group and went to the United States. On that trip, he saw Niagara Falls. That moment was just like the one when he first saw the tightrope walker. Charles knew that he had to cross the enormous falls on a tightrope.

The great day was June 30, 1859. Charles's team put up a rope that was three inches (7.62 cm) thick and 1,100 feet (335.28 m) long. The cord sagged in the middle, dropping more than 100 feet (30.48 m) as it went across the roaring falls. At its highest point, it was close to 300 feet (91.44 m) above the falls! Thousands of people came to watch this daring **feat**. No one had ever tried anything like it before.

Charles made it across safely, but he wanted to do more. He made more trips across Niagara Falls. Each time, he had a new trick to please the huge crowds who watched him. One time, he put a chair on the tightrope and then stood on the wobbling chair. Another time, he pushed a wheelbarrow across the rope. Charles even walked across the tightrope blindfolded. On one of his most amazing trips, he carried a little stove. Halfway across the falls, he stopped, cooked some eggs, and ate them!

His trips across Niagara Falls made Charles famous. Later, he performed around Europe. He did not **retire** until he was 68 years old.

stage name: a fake name used by a performer
feat: an act of skill
retire: to end one's career

Balancing Act

Answer the questions.

1. When did Charles Blondin decide to become a tightrope walker?

   A. He decided when he saw Niagara Falls.

   B. He decided when he became an orphan at the age of nine.

   C. He decided when he saw a tightrope walker at a circus when he was five years old.

   D. He decided after he joined a circus for the first time.

2. Which of the following is not a fact from the story?

   A. Charles Blondin pushed a wheelbarrow across Niagara Falls on a rope.

   B. The rope he used was 1,100 feet (335.28 m) long.

   C. Charles Blondin only crossed Niagara Falls because someone dared him.

   D. Charles Blondin did not retire until he was 68 years old.

3. Read the following sentence and answer the question.

   Thousands of people came to watch this daring feat.

   Which other phrase could the author have used in place of this *daring feat*?

   A. this amazing story   **B.** this dangerous act

   C. this boring event   **D.** none of the above

4. Which of the following is not talked about in the story?

   A. the time Charles Blondin crossed a tightrope carrying another person on his back

   B. the time Charles Blondin cooked eggs and ate them on a tightrope

   C. the time Charles Blondin walked blindfolded on a tightrope

   D. the time Charles Blondin stood on a chair on a tightrope

5. Circle the irregular past tense verbs.

cooked	saw	stopped
stood	started	took
ate	wanted	liked

6. Why do you think that some people like to do dangerous things? Write your answer on another sheet of paper. Ask a teacher or classmate to read your essay. Then, revise and rewrite your essay.

Sandstone Giant

People stand and look at the huge rock. It is more than 1,000 feet (304.8 m) tall. If someone walks all of the way around the huge rock, he will walk almost six miles (9.66 km)! *Uluru* is the native name of the giant rock. It is found in the center of Australia. It is also known as Ayers Rock. Many old drawings are found on the rock. People tell **legends** about how the rock came to be. One story says that **serpents** had fights around the rock. Their weapons made the marks and caves on the sides of the rock.

Scientists think that Uluru was under the sea 500 million years ago. It sits in the middle of the **outback**. The rock has many caves. Small trees and grass grow on parts of the rock. Many animals live there. There are lizards, mice, kangaroos, and birds.

The rounded rock looks like it was made by humans. It has long folds across its sides. The red sandstone seems to change colors in the sunlight. This is because of the way light hits the folds. The rock turns purple and blue. It does not rain much in the outback. When it rains on Uluru, many waterfalls come down the sides of the sandstone giant.

Uluru is now a national park. People used to ride camels to the rock. Trucks and planes now take visitors to the rock. People can climb the rock. But, the native people do not like it. The rock has special meaning to them. Some people take small rocks home. Many rocks are sent back. Some people think that they will have bad luck if they keep the rocks.

legend: a story from the past told again and again
serpent: snake-like creature
outback: rural area in Australia

Sandstone Giant

People often stand looking at the huge sandstone rock. It rises more than 1,000 feet (304.8 m) from the floor of the desert. It is almost six miles (9.66 km) around the rock! When the sun sets on the rock, the red sandstone seems to change colors. The rock turns purple and blue. This place is Uluru. It is found in Australia.

Uluru is the native name of the giant rock. It is also known as Ayers Rock. Many ancient drawings are found on the rock. People tell **legends** about how the rock came to be. One story says that **serpents** had fights around the rock. Their weapons made the marks that are now the folds, grooves, and caves in Uluru.

Scientists think that Uluru was under the sea 500 million years ago. It sits in the middle of the **outback**. The rock has many caves. Small trees and grass grow on parts of the rock. Many animals live there. There are lizards, mice, kangaroos, and birds.

The rounded rock looks like it was made by humans, with long folds across its sides. The rock seems to change colors in the sunlight. This is because of the way light hits the folds. It does not rain much in the outback. When it rains on Uluru, many waterfalls come down the sides of the sandstone giant.

Uluru is now a national park. People used to ride camels to the rock. Trucks and planes now take visitors to the rock. People can climb the rock. But, the native people do not like it. The rock has special meaning to them. Some people take small rocks home. Many are sent back because some people think that they will have bad luck if they keep the rocks.

legend: a story from the past told again and again
serpent: snake-like creature
outback: rural area in Australia

Sandstone Giant

People often stand looking at the huge sandstone rock. It rises more than 1,000 feet (304.8 m) from the floor of the desert. If someone decides to walk all of the way around the huge rock, he will walk almost six miles (9.66 km)! When the sun sets on the rock, the red sandstone seems to change colors. The rock turns purple and blue. This magical place is Uluru, and it is found in the middle of Australia.

Uluru is the native name of the giant rock. It is also known as Ayers Rock. Many ancient drawings are found on the rock and in its caves. Native people tell **legends** about this strange place and how the rock came to be. One story says that **serpents** had great battles around the rock. Their weapons made the scars that are now the folds, grooves, and caves in Uluru.

Scientists think that Uluru was under the sea 500 million years ago. Now, it sits in the middle of the **outback**. The rocky sides of Uluru have many caves. Small trees and grass grow in some places on the rock. Many birds and animals live there. There are also lizards, hopping mice, and kangaroos. Parrots and falcons also live on the giant sandstone rock.

The rock looks almost like it was made by humans, with long ripples, or folds across its sides. During the day, the rock seems to change colors. This is because of the way light hits its folds and caves. It does not rain very much in the outback. But, when it does rain on Uluru, hundreds of waterfalls pour down the flowing sides of the sandstone giant.

Uluru is now a national park. People used to ride camels to the rock, and now trucks and planes take visitors to the rock. People can climb the rock, but the native people do not like visitors to do so. The rock has special meaning to their culture. Some people take small rocks home. Many are sent back because some people think they'll have bad luck if they keep the rocks.

legend: a story from the past told again and again
serpent: snake-like creature
outback: rural area in serpents in Australia

Name _____

3.RI.1, 3.RI.4, 3.RI.7, 3.L.1, 3.L.2

Sandstone Giant

Answer the questions.

1. Read the following sentence and answer the question.

   People tell legends about this strange place and how the rock came to be.

   Which word means the opposite of *strange*?

   A. mysterious

   B. awful

   C. weird

   D. ordinary

2. Who named the rock *Uluru*? Write your answer in a complete sentence.

   _____

   _____

3. Which of the following is not a feature of Uluru?

   A. It changes colors at sunset.

   B. It has caves with ancient drawings.

   C. It has a lake on top.

   D. It is made of sandstone.

Write **T** for true or **F** for false.

4. _____ Uluru is made of granite.

5. _____ Uluru's cave drawings were made by aliens.

6. _____ There is a story that says that the caves on Uluru were made by serpents.

7. Circle three compound words from the story.

   sandstone   serpent   waterfalls

   middle   human   outback

8. On another sheet of paper, write your version of a legend that explains how the ripples on Uluru came to be.

© Carson-Dellosa · CD-104615 · Differentiated Reading for Comprehension   55

A Sea without Fish

A body of water in the desert sounds good. But the Dead Sea does not have water you can drink. The Dead Sea is the saltiest place on Earth. It is really a lake. It is called a sea because it does not have freshwater.

Why is the Dead Sea so salty? It is about a quarter mile (0.4 km) below sea level. A long time ago, salt water went into the Dead Sea. Now, water from a river goes into the lake. The water has no **outlet**. Some of the water **evaporates** in the hot sun. Salt is left behind.

Scientists say that the Dead Sea is sinking. It has sunk as much as 13 inches (33.02 cm) in some years. People are using more water from the river. Less freshwater enters the lake every year.

Lakes are filled with life. But, the Dead Sea lives up to its name. Nothing lives there. There are no plants. No birds or animals can drink the water. If fish from the river swim into the Dead Sea by mistake, they die. The water kills almost everything. It is saltier than ocean water.

People like to visit this lake. It is hot and sunny. There are hotels and beaches. People float in the Dead Sea. The salty water holds people up as if they were lying on rafts! It is harder to stand than it is to float. Some **tourists** even like to read books as they float on top of the water. They are covered with salt when they come out of the water.

outlet: an opening or exit
evaporate: to change into vapor or gas
tourist: visitor

A Sea without Fish

Water in the middle of a desert sounds good. But the Dead Sea does not hold water that people or animals can drink. The Dead Sea is the saltiest place on Earth. It is really a lake. It is called a sea because it does not have freshwater.

Why is the Dead Sea so salty? It sits almost a quarter mile (0.4 km) below sea level. More than three million years ago, salt water from the Mediterranean Sea went into the Dead Sea. Water flows into the Dead Sea today from a river. The water has no **outlet**. Some of the water **evaporates** in the hot sun. Salt is left behind.

Scientists say that the Dead Sea is sinking. It has sunk as much as 13 inches (33.02 cm) in some years. People are using more water from the river. Less freshwater enters the lake every year.

Lakes are usually filled with plants and animals. But, the Dead Sea lives up to its name. Nothing can stay alive there. There is no seaweed. No birds or animals can drink its salty water. If fish from the river swim into the Dead Sea by mistake, they die quickly. The water kills almost everything. It is at least seven times saltier than ocean water.

People like to visit this lake. The weather is hot and sunny. There are hotels and beaches. People float in the Dead Sea. The salty water holds people's bodies up as if they were lying on rafts! It is actually harder to stand in the Dead Sea than it is to float. Some **tourists** even like to read books as they float on top of the water. When they come out, they are covered with salt.

outlet: an opening or exit
evaporate: to change into vapor or gas
tourist: visitor

A Sea without Fish

A big body of water in the middle of a desert sounds great, but the Dead Sea does not hold water that people or animals can drink. This big body of water between the countries of Jordan and Israel is the saltiest place on Earth. It is not really a sea at all; it is a lake. But, it is called a sea because it does not have freshwater.

Why is the Dead Sea so salty? It sits almost a quarter mile (0.4 km) below sea level. More than three million years ago, salt water from the Mediterranean Sea poured into a deep opening to form the Dead Sea. Today, water flows into the Dead Sea from the Jordan River and several streams. But, the water has no **outlet**. Some of the water **evaporates** in the hot sun. Salt and other minerals are left behind.

Scientists say that the Dead Sea is actually sinking. During some years, the Dead Sea has sunk as much as 13 inches (33.02 cm). And, people are using more water from the Jordan River, so less freshwater enters the Dead Sea every year. As it sinks lower and receives less freshwater, evaporation causes it to become saltier and saltier.

Lakes are usually filled with life. But, the Dead Sea lives up to its name. Nothing can stay alive there. There is no seaweed. No birds or animals can drink its salty water. If fish from the Jordan River swim into the Dead Sea by mistake, they die quickly. The water kills almost everything. It is at least seven times saltier than ocean water.

People like to visit this strange, quiet lake. The weather is hot and sunny. There are hotels and beaches. The people float on the surface of the Dead Sea. People who have been swimming in an ocean and a pool will notice that it is easier to float in an ocean. That is because of the salt in ocean water. Because the Dead Sea has so much salt, it is hard to swim in it. The salt holds people's bodies up as if they were lying on rafts! It is actually harder to stand in the Dead Sea than it is to float. Some **tourists** even like to read books as they float on top of the water. When they come out, they are covered with salt.

outlet: an opening or exit
evaporate: to change into vapor or gas
tourist: visitor

A Sea without Fish

1. Read the following sentence from the story and answer the question.

   But, the Dead Sea lives up to its name.

   Why does the author say this?

   A. Nothing can live in the Dead Sea.

   B. The Dead Sea is really a lake.

   C. People cannot go into the water of the Dead Sea.

   D. The Dead Sea is too quiet.

2. Which of the following is not explained in the story?

   A. how the Dead Sea became so salty

   B. that the Dead Sea is sinking even lower

   C. what happens to fish that swim into the Dead Sea

   D. how people use minerals from the Dead Sea in spa treatments

3. Rewrite the following sentence from the story so that it is correct.

   Some tourists even likes to read books as he float on top of the water.

   _____

   _____

4. Which of the following defines *outlet* as it is used in the story?

   A. a place to buy clothing

   B. a place to plug in a lamp

   C. a place for water to go after it has flowed into a lake

   D. a way to show feelings

5. In the words *dead* and *sea,* the vowel pair *ea* makes different sounds. Circle the words that have the same vowel sound as *dead.* Underline the words that have the same vowel sound as *sea.*

peach	ahead	pea
eagle	treat	ready
leap	meat	bread

6. Would you like to be a tourist and visit the Dead Sea? Why or why not? Write your answer on another sheet of paper.

"Ice" to Meet You

How would you like to get your milk in big, frozen blocks? That is a part of life in Verkhoyansk, Russia. It is one of the coldest places in the northern **hemisphere**. The little town of 1,800 people is in Siberia. One day, the temperature was -90°F (-67.78°C)!

What is life there like in the winter? If people go outside in winter, they will hear a whooshing sound. It sounds like rice being poured out of a bag. It is the sound of their breath turning into ice crystals. The crystals fall to the ground in front of them. The native people call this sound "the whisper of the stars."

The cold makes life difficult. It is so cold that trees can break and houses can split. If people drink hot tea, their teeth can even crack.

Winter there is dark, as well as cold. On some days, the only daylight is a faint light, low in the sky. You may think that no one would want to live in such a cold place.

In the past, the town was used as a prison. People were sent to live there as punishment.

Other people are from tribes who have lived there for thousands of years. There are groups of **nomads** who live in the mountains. They are hunters. They also raise **herds** of reindeer.

They say that it is warmer in the mountains than it is in the town. That is because the town is in a **valley**. The coldest air comes into the valley, and the mountains hold it there. There is no wind to move it. The air in the town is dry and cold.

People of the town live with the cold. They get blocks of ice from the river. They melt them on their stoves for water. They buy their milk in frozen disks. That's life in Verkhoyansk!

---

hemisphere: a half of the earth

nomad: a person who moves from place to place

raise: to breed and care for

valley: a place between mountains

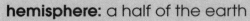

"Ice" to Meet You

How would you like to have your milk delivered in frozen disks? That is a part of life in Verkhoyansk, Russia, one of the coldest places in the northern **hemisphere**. The little town of 1,800 people is in Siberia. On its coldest winter day on record, the temperature was -90°F (-67.78°C)!

What is life there like in the winter? In winter a whooshing sound can be heard. It sounds like rice being poured out of a bag. It is the sound of people's breath turning into ice crystals. The crystals fall to the ground in front of them.

The cold makes life difficult. It is so cold that trees can explode and houses can split. If people drink hot tea, their teeth can crack. And, if people go outside and pour the tea out of their cups, it can freeze before it hits the ground.

Winter there is dark, as well as cold. On some days, the only daylight is a low, faint light. You may think that no one would want to live in such a cold place. In the past, the town was used as a prison. People were sent to live there as punishment.

But, other people are from tribes who have lived there for thousands of years. There are groups of **nomads** who live in the mountains. They **raise** reindeer. They say that it is actually warmer in the mountains than it is in the town! That is because the town is in a **valley** between the mountains. The coldest air comes into the valley, and the mountains hold it there. The air in the town is like the air inside a freezer. It is dry and cold.

The people of the town have found ways to deal with the cold. They get blocks of ice from the river. They melt them on their stoves for water. They buy their milk in frozen disks. It is easy to carry the milk home and melt the disks when they are needed. That's life in Verkhoyansk!

hemisphere: a half of the earth
nomad: a person who moves from place to place
raise: to breed and care for
valley: a place between mountains

"Ice" to Meet You

How would you like to have your milk delivered in big, frozen blocks? That is a part of life in Verkhoyansk, Russia, one of the coldest places in the northern **hemisphere**. The little town of 1,800 people is in Siberia. On its coldest winter day on record, the town **endured** a temperature of -90°F (-67.78°C)!

What is life there like in the winter? If people go outside in the winter, they will hear a whooshing sound, like the sound of rice being poured out of a bag. It is the sound of their breath turning into ice crystals. The crystals fall to the ground in front of them.

The temperature makes life difficult. Sometimes, it is so cold that the trees explode and the foundations of houses split. If people drink hot tea in Verkhoyansk, their teeth can crack. And, if people go outside and pour the tea out of their cups, it can freeze before it hits the ground.

Winter there is dark, as well as cold. On some days, the only daylight is a low, faint light in the sky. You may think that no one would want to live in such a cold place. When Russia was ruled by czars, the town was used as a prison. People were sent to live there as punishment.

There are groups of **nomads** who live in the mountains. They raise herds of reindeer. They say that it is actually warmer in the mountains than it is in the town. That is because the town is in a **valley** between the mountains. The coldest air comes into the valley, and the mountains hold it there. If there is no wind to move it, the air in the town is like the air inside a freezer—still, dry, and cold.

But, the people of the town have found ways to deal with the cold. They gather blocks of ice from the river for water. And, they buy their milk in large, frozen disks. It is easy to carry them home and melt them when milk is needed. That's life in Verkhoyansk!

hemisphere: a half of the earth
endure: to undergo or suffer
nomad: a person who moves from place to place
valley: a place between mountains

"Ice" to Meet You

Answer the questions.

1. Write the comparative and superlative forms of each adjective. The first one is done for you.

   warm   _____warmer_____   _____warmest_____

   cold   _____   _____

   dark   _____   _____

   easy   _____   _____

2. Where is Verkhoyansk?

   A. Alaska   **B.** Russia   **C.** Siberia   **D.** B. and C.

3. How cold can it get in Verkhoyansk? Write your answer in a complete sentence.

   _____

   _____

4. Circle three adjectives that describe winter life in Verkhoyansk.

   inviting   luxurious   difficult   tropical

   frigid   busy   dark   humid

5. What is the best description of why it is so cold in Verkhoyansk?

   A. It is so cold and dark in the wintertime because a person's breath freezes in the air.

   B. It is so cold because the town is in a valley and the mountains trap the cold air over the town.

   C. It is so cold because the wind blows so hard that it blows apart houses.

   D. It is so cold because Verkhoyansk is in Siberia and all of Siberia is just as cold as this town.

6. Which of the following is not true?

   A. If you drink something hot in Verkhoyansk during the winter, your teeth can crack.

   B. In Verkhoyansk, some house foundations crack in the winter.

   C. It is colder in the mountains outside Verkhoyansk than it is in the town.

   D. Verkhoyansk was used as a prison.

7. Would you like to visit Verkhoyansk? Why or why not? Write your answer on another sheet of paper.

Answer Key

Page 7
1. D; 2. A puggle is a baby platypus. 3. C; 4. B; 5. It has little pads inside its bill that grind its food. 6. D; 7. Answers will vary. 8. Answers will vary.

Page 11
1. C; 2. B; 3. D; 4. 10 feet (3.05 m); 5. 3 feet (91.44 cm); 6. frog-jumping; 7. Answers will vary.

Page 15
1. D; 2. B; 3. F; 4. F; 5. T; 6. D; 7. B; 8. Answers will vary.

Page 19
1. disapprove, to not approve of something; 2. disable, to make unusable; 3. disagree, to not agree; 4. disobey, to not obey; 5. The Marfa lights get their name from the town in which they are seen. 6. A; 7. F; 8. T; 9. T; 10. T; 11. lights from boats; 12. Answers will vary.

Page 23
1. C; 2. Answers will vary but may include: Airplanes today are not circular with domed ceilings and portholes. 3. C; 4. plumber, knife, island, debt, wrap, climb, hoe, castle; 5. C; 6. C; 7. Answers will vary.

Page 27
1. Japan; 2. Europe; 3. plane; 4. 1959; 5. T; 6. F; 7. T; 8. T; 9. D; 10. Answers will vary.

Page 31
1. C; 2. F; 3. T; 4. T; 5. Answers will vary but may include: cook, talk on the phone, learn new things, listen to people, know when people are happy or sad, do chores; 6. paint, learn, build, crawl, walk; 7. Answers will vary. 8. Answers will vary.

Page 35
1. D; 2. C; 3. A; 4. B; 5. D; 6. built, will launch, fly; 7. Answers will vary.

Page 39
1. A; 2. F; 3. T; 4. F; 5. C; 6. poor, sickly, small; 7. C; 8. Answers will vary but may include: Wilma's mother took care of her when she was sick. Wilma's brothers and sisters made sure she kept on her braces. 9. Answers will vary.

Page 43
1. T; 2. F; 3. T; 4. F; 5. D; 6. B; 7. A; 8. teacher, one who teaches, writer, one who writes, leader, one who leads, painter, one who paints, ruler, one who rules, baker, one who bakes; 9. Answers will vary.

Page 47
1. C; 2. D; 3. happiness, the state of being happy, darkness, the state of being dark, loneliness, the state of being lonely, illness, the state of being ill; 4. 1840; 5. laws; 6. nine days; 7. Answers will vary.

Page 51
1. C; 2. C; 3. B; 4. A; 5. saw, stood, took, ate; 6. Answers will vary.

Page 55
1. D; 2. The native Australians named the rock Uluru. 3. C; 4. F; 5. F; 6. F; 7. sandstone, waterfalls, outback; 8. Answers will vary.

Page 59
1. A; 2. D; 3. Some tourists even like to read books as they float on top of the water. 4. C; 5. circled words: ahead, ready bread; underlined words: peach, pea, eagle, treat, leap, meat; 6. Answers will vary.

Page 63
1. colder, coldest, darker, darkest, easier, easiest; 2. D; 3. Answers will vary but should include the temperature. 4. difficult, frigid, dark; 5. B; 6. C; 7. Answers will vary.

Notes

_____

_____

_____

_____

_____

_____